Reinventing
By Mik~ ~

DATE DUE

2

I wish I could devote a whole chapter in dedication to my wife Andrea. She has put "normal" back into my life more than anyone ever has. Andrea, you are the kind of person that this world is begging for. You are amazing!

I also want to dedicate this book to my children. You have no idea how much you mean to me. I love every moment we get to be together!

Introduction		**7**
Chapter 1	**The picture of normal**	**11**
Chapter 2	**Not the only one**	**17**
Chapter 3	**Loretta**	**23**
Chapter 4	**Spirals**	**31**
Chapter 5	**I Cut**	**37**
Chapter 6	**Black out**	**45**
Chapter 7	**I know he is using me**	**53**
Chapter 8	**Sex isn't ice cream**	**61**
Chapter 9	**Country club skills**	**67**
Chapter 10	**Who can you trust?**	**77**
Chapter 11	**Forgive who?**	**87**
Chapter 12	**Hurt people hurt people**	**95**
Chapter 13	**My Bad**	**103**
Chapter 14	**Flip the script**	**111**
Chapter 15	**Voices in my head**	**125**
Chapter 16	**Harold and his pitchfork**	**133**
Chapter 17	**I hate Christians**	**143**
Chapter 18	**Chasing Harold**	**151**

Introduction

Was it when I came down stairs one night to see my dad kicking my mom in the stomach while she was pregnant with my sister? Was it when he left and didn't call for a couple of years? Was it when one of my babysitter's boyfriends punched me in the face because he was too drunk to know that I was only nine years old? I'm just trying to figure out when my normal changed.

Go look at your washing machine in your laundry room. There is a setting on it called normal. You can choose heavy, light or normal. Wouldn't it be great if life came with an option like that? No matter how messed up things got, you could switch it to normal.

I feel like my whole life I've been adjusting my normal, just trying to make sense out of a bunch of pain. I used to be so jealous of other people who I thought had a normal life; only to find out their life was not normal either.

I don't think I have ever met anyone normal. Isn't it funny that we think everyone else is sane except ourselves? Like we are the only ones experiencing the stuff that we are going through?

What really is normal? Is there such a thing? Normal is the ideal. It is the anchor, the standard, I guess. Our world changes so fast that I don't think normal has kept up with it. What does a normal teenager look like? What is a normal parent? What is a normal American? What in the world is normal?

Just the other day I was speaking at a school, and a girl told me that she had a "normal life," and that she was not like a lot of the other kids who had "bad lives." Then she told me that her parents were divorced, and she never talked to her dad. That was her normal. It got me thinking. Maybe normal is different for everyone.

When did your normal change? When did life punch you in the stomach? How did you handle it? How did you adjust? Did you get sad? Mad? Did you tell anyone? People do crazy things when their normal changes. It doesn't have to be some big thing that happened to you to make your normal change. Sometimes it is just everyday stuff, like growing up and not seeing things from the bubble of childhood anymore.

I remember when I was about eight years old, I heard about a man and his wife who were arrested for severely beating their daughter. They would hang her by her feet and beat her. They starved her and would not let her out of the house. I remember it having a profound effect on me. It was the first time in my life I'd heard of anything like that. Think about how many times you have heard things or seen things that made your normal change.

After about six years of doing R5 Productions and talking to thousands of kids, I wanted to write a book that would answer many frequently asked questions. This is an attempt to help you pick up the pieces of your life and do something great with them.

I don't claim to be an expert but I want to share with you some things that have helped me along the way.

I want to breathe courage and hope into some of the most amazing people I have ever been privileged to rub shoulders with... American teenagers.

I'm often asked, "Who are your heroes?" I have to tell you that my answer is probably not normal either. It's not the great athlete or the brilliant scholar that impresses me the most. It is you. It's the person reading this book, going along in life until something happened. An event or series of events may have changed what you used to call normal. Through the tears and the anger you have attempted to reinvent your normal. You are my hero.

It's May of 1974 and I'm walking up the hill to my house in a suburb just south of Boston. It is a beautiful spring day. The sun is out and everything seems normal, and why wouldn't it? We are a very normal neighborhood. We have normal people, normal dogs, and normal cats. We are a very normal-looking neighborhood.

As we get closer to my house, we see Mrs. Schultz. She is washing the side of her house with a hose. She does that every spring. She was the first one in the neighborhood to get aluminum siding.

Tommy Murray and his dad are playing catch in the front yard. Mr. Stanton is on his front porch as usual. He is pretty old.

I am almost to my house, and you can see Mrs. Lambosi getting out of her car with groceries. They have five kids, and their eldest boy is a few years older than I and is a good friend of mine.

Then there's Harold. He is in his garden. Every year he has this huge garden. Harold has to be pushing 80. Everyone in our town knows this guy. People are always yelling out his name when they drive by. He just yells "Yo!" really loud. He never even looks up at them. Harold is a World War I veteran who never got married. He lives with his older sister Mamee, who also never got married. I'm sorry, I don't care how old I get I'm never living with my sister.

Harold and Mamee own the house to the east of us. The lady to the west is Anna B. She seemed to know everything I was going to do before I did it. She kept my mom "in the loop" about everything I did. Thanks, Anna.

Just to the north of her lived Jack Felton. He just graduated from college and was working as an engineer for the city. It's a pretty nice job for someone in our normal neighborhood.

Next door to Anna lived the Smiths. They had five kids, all boys, except one girl who was named after the mom. How normal is that?

Around the corner was a group of houses with many kids my age. We played street hockey for hours up there. Steve, Joey, Michael, Patrick and Paul – a bunch of good guys whom I hung around quite a bit. All had normal lives.

Our neighborhood was your typical suburban Boston neighborhood. Everyone went to church. We were mostly Catholic, with a few Protestant Christians thrown in there.

If you took a snapshot of our neighborhood in 1974, you would say, "That is a very normal neighborhood, for real."

Then there was our family. We were probably the one wrinkle in that normal neighborhood scenario.

My parents got a divorce in 1969. I remember feeling kind of weird about that. We were the only ones in our neighborhood at the time.

Even though my mom worked hard as a nurse, we did not have a whole lot of money. It didn't help that the Lambosis were very rich and they lived right across the street from us. Mr. Lambosi was one of those self-made man types. He owned a couple of businesses and also worked for one of the utility companies.

We were the odd ones. I couldn't tell if people were annoyed with us or felt sorry for us. Maybe a little bit of both. Irritated because we were interrupting their "precious" normal.

The picture of normal had a stain on it... and it was the Donahues.

Apply this to my head

Have you ever felt different from everyone else around you?

How did it make you feel?

List any events in your family or community that might have changed your normal, or what you thought normal should be.

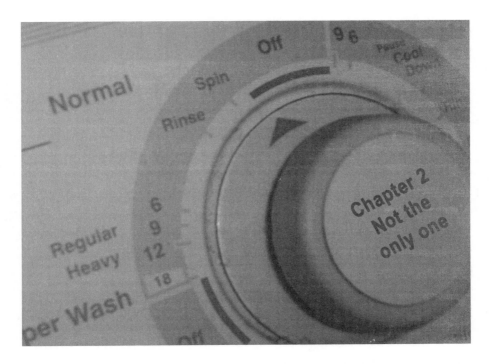

Chapter 2
Not the only one

Let's fast forward to 1981. The picture has changed quite a bit in seven years.

Mrs. Schultz doesn't come out of her house anymore because her husband left her for another man.

Tommy Murray hasn't seen his dad in a couple of years because he finally divorced his wife. I knew they were having problems because Tommy's dad would stop over at our house drunk and hit on my mom.

Everyone stays away from Mr. Stanton now because he was arrested for being a pervert. He even tried to mess with my sister.

The older Lambosi son declared that he was gay and has been living with his partner ever since. Mr. Lambosi was not happy and rarely talked with his son. Ronny later died of AIDS.

My friend Steve, one of the guys I played hockey with, committed suicide. To this day no one knows why.

The Smith's only daughter allegedly stole a bunch of money from her parents. Apparently she forged checks using her mom's name since they had the same name.

Jack Felton turned out to be one of the biggest drug dealers in our town. He sold pounds of marijuana from the house he rented to the north of us.

Then there was Harold. In the last eight years I watched this man do some of the most bizarre things that anyone could do.

I knew he wasn't normal when he would urinate in jars out in his garage and save it. I'm really not making this up. On breezy days he would throw the urine on the side of his yard when my mom had the windows open. I can't even describe to you how nasty that smelled.

Harold was unbelievable. We had three crab apple trees in our yard. Many of the branches extended over the fence into his yard. Every August there were rotten apples everywhere. Harold would collect all the apples that fell into his yard and put them in buckets around his property. Then he'd wait until he heard people in our backyard and then randomly throw them over the fence at us.

I thought that was the funniest thing in the world. I would

go back there sometimes and make noise so he would chuck them at me. One day all my friends were in my back yard. We were getting ready to take off somewhere on our bikes, and all of a sudden we were being pelted with apples.

My mother was there, so I asked her if we could throw some back. She said, "Yes, but don't hit him." (Yeah, right!) You should have seen his eyes when all eight of us popped our heads over that fence and started firing. I laughed about that for years. You will read more about Harold later.

Let's just say that the Donahues were not the only flaw on the portrait of our normal quiet little street south of Boston. Behind the masks were people whose lives were different than they appeared. I have a feeling our neighborhood was not the only one.

My normal changed quite a bit in that time as well. I began to use drugs and alcohol when I was in junior high. By the time I was a junior in high school, my relationship with my mom had gotten really bad, so I moved out of my house.

I was living in an apartment on the other side of town. I stayed in school and tried to work odd jobs to survive. Not exactly what most people would call "normal."

In the following chapters I am going to try to describe my journey in reinventing my normal.

Apply this to my head

When did you notice that you were not the only one in your world with problems?

Why do we tend to think that we are the only one going through hard times?

Do you think people wear masks in order to appear "normal"?

What mask or masks do you wear?

Why can wearing masks be dangerous?

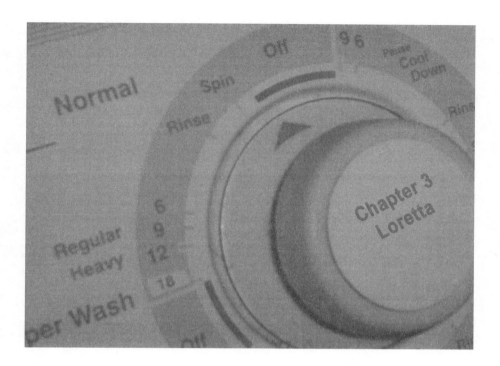

Chapter 3
Loretta

I was nine years old when my mom told me something very strange. One of our babysitters would not be coming over anymore because she was on drugs. Her name was Loretta and I liked her. I had a series of questions for my mom that I don't think she was ready to answer. "Why do people do drugs?" "What are drugs?" "What do they do to you?" I asked questions that a nine-year-old would ask. Most importantly, "What was going to happen to my friend Loretta?"

A sixteen-year-old girl just told me that when she was about seven years old she was riding in the car with her mother and two sisters ages three and one. The car got a flat tire and the mom left the kids in the car by themselves.

A couple of hours later she figured out that her mom wasn't coming back. So, carrying the one-year-old and holding the hand of the three-year-old she bravely walked a couple of miles to her aunt's house. There she found her mother, sitting at the kitchen table getting drunk.

For ten minutes this girl told me story after story of how she had to take over and raise her two sisters because her mom was always drunk.

So explain to me what reasons this sixteen-year-old girl would have to turn down an offer for street drugs? I'm not trying to give anyone an excuse, I'm just asking a question.

What is she supposed to do?

How does a young girl deal with that kind of pain? If she wants the pain to go away, she might try doing something that will make her feel better. She could try any number of artificial ways to medicate herself.

Let's face it; doctors wouldn't prescribe drugs if they didn't work. Pain medication helps many people. However, there is a limit.

Pain medicine does take away pain, but never the problem.

There has been a great deal written and many discussions over what experts are calling the "drug culture" today.

I'm not an expert, but I believe that a "drug culture" exists because a "pain culture" exists.

In my twenty-something years of dealing with young people, I have never heard so much pain as I have in the last six years.

Pain often leads to self-medication. Drugs, alcohol, cutting, bad relationships, eating disorders, fits of anger, etc… are just some of the ways that people are trying to deal with the stress of life on their own. I can totally relate to that.

I was nineteen years old and in the Air Force. Everyday I put rum in my coffee. I was an alcoholic. By noon I was pretty wasted. I would go home from work and just go to bed. I was self- medicating. I was trying to make all the pain of growing up the way I did go away. My normal was all messed up and I didn't have the tools to handle it.

I wouldn't allow myself to feel the pain because I didn't know how to fix it.

Maybe that's why you don't want to feel your own personal pain? Perhaps it seems hopeless and you don't know how else to fix it.

I couldn't bring my dad back. I couldn't get my mom to like me. I couldn't get rid of the memories of all the bad stuff that I saw and did, so I drank and did drugs in an effort to take away some of the pain.

That is the problem with self-medication. It is only a temporary solution, very temporary. Drugs solve the immediate problem of pain. A cure takes longer.

Have you ever had a cut that got infected? You have to pull the scab off to clean it out. You can't just put a band-aid on it or take a pain pill. Cleaning out the wound is a very painful process. Think about emotional pain and self-medication in the same way. You have this infection that is causing more pain. Self-medication may cover up the problem for a while, but the infection gets worse. You have to go through the immediate pain of taking off the scab and cleaning it to get rid of the pain permanently.

Emotional pain has to be dealt with the same way. Once you take care of the infection, you will begin to heal and you will no longer need the medication.

One of the differences between people who end up living out their dreams and those who resent them is the ability to properly handle emotional pain, especially how they handle it in their teenage years.

I have watched lives take incredibly wrong turns as a result of the death of a loved one, the ending of a romantic relationship, not making an athletic team, a parents' divorce, or even a friend moving out of state.

Some of my personal heroes have endured these same hardships without self-destructing. The old saying

"What doesn't kill you can make you stronger" is really true.

While I was in Boston a couple of years ago, I ran into Loretta at the grocery store. She was now in her forties. She told me that after years of going in and out of rehab, she was finally dealing with the issues that made her do drugs in the first place.

She talked about her abusive, alcoholic step-dad and other painful things that made her self-medicate. I was really glad that she was finally getting the help that she needed. However, I couldn't help thinking that she wasted about twenty-five years of her life trying to make the pain go away and it never did. It just got worse. Loretta went through many painful moments before she realized she needed to go to the root of the pain.

I hope it doesn't take you that long. I hope that you will be able to identify what is causing your pain. It won't be easy. I hope you have the courage to continue reading.

Note: There are many people who take specific medication for depression or other emotional disorders. When I refer to "self-medication" I am not talking about those drugs. There are certain situations that require management tools for depression and other disorders. If you think you are one of those people, talk to someone who can help.

Apply this to my head

Write down a list of the things that you are trying to medicate. Be specific. Write them all down.

What have you been doing to make the pain go away? (Drugs, alcohol, cutting, abusive relationships, etc.)

You need to admit that the way you have been dealing with it is not really helping. This is hard because it might have been making you feel better at times. It might numb you to the pain, but it could be doing other damage and getting worse. Write down some ways it is getting worse.

Spirals are fascinating. Have you ever looked into a spiraling seashell? It seems like they go on forever; that if your eyes were stronger, they'd see the spiral continue down out of sight. Only from far away does it seem to end and come to a point.

A friend of mine wrote an e-mail describing a spiral of her own.

Mike, I need help. I'm at the bottom of a long downward spiral. Maybe it isn't the bottom. I hope it is. I can't imagine falling any further.

When you knew me I was fourteen. At that point I was a virgin. I'd never even had a sip of alcohol. Now, I don't even remember all the stupid things I've done. Everyone knows I'm the party girl. I've been called a "slut", a "pothead" and worse, but I was always like, screw them, I never cared what others thought.

But to be honest, I'd be ashamed to meet that girl you knew. I'm jealous of her innocence. I can't get that back, can I? I hate you. You always make me cry when you speak, and now I'm crying just writing you! J/K you know. I'll always remember how you believed in me.

I'm writing you because I can't remember what that girl was like. I know she had issues and frustrations. I know she wanted to be different. But I want you to tell her something if you meet her when you're traveling. Tell her the grass isn't greener over here.

Tell her the thrill is gone the next morning… and it never comes back. Tell her I hate the woman I've become and I would give anything to be her again. You taught us about downward spirals. How hard it is to stop once you start. I know it is never too late to change, but I don't think I ever will.

She's eighteen. She sounds like she's thirty. She sounds like her life is over – when in truth it's just beginning. If she was crying writing it, it makes me want to cry reading it. Because I remember her when she was fourteen.

If you're reading this, and you are that fourteen-year-old girl, I have a message from a friend of mine.

The grass isn't greener over there. She said the thrill is gone in the morning and never comes back.

I know what that's like. You buy into a lifestyle for the thrill and then stick around to stay numb.

One winter my brother David, cousin Billy and I were at

my grandpa's house near Plymouth, Massachusetts. (Is it me, or does everyone have a cousin Billy?) Anyhow, they lived near these massive cranberry bogs owned by Ocean Spray. During the winter, Ocean Spray would flood them, turning them into vast fields of ice.

The wind would come in off the Atlantic and just whip across these ice fields. We'd get skating fast and then open our coats with our arms, basically wind skating in sub-zero weather. To stop, all we would do is close our arms and wrap our coats back around us.

My brother was seven, so he didn't weigh much, and the wind got a hold of him. I can still see him now, arms holding his coat out, the wind just driving him forward... screaming at the top of his lungs!

He was going so fast that he got scared and wouldn't put his arms down, even though he was heading toward a part of the bog that wasn't frozen. He was scared, and screaming, and seven, and going really fast.

Splash!

The water was only waist deep. But he was so cold he was miserable.

I wonder how many people you know are doing the same thing. They opened their coat in the wind for a rush, and now they can't stop. Sure they could, all they have to do is close their coat. But for some reason, it never comes to mind.

They can even see the water up ahead. Sometimes they know they're going to crash. Why don't they close their coat? Why don't they stop? Momentum builds, and as speed increases, you know that somehow, someday, one way or another you're going to come to a sudden stop.

But we were talking about spirals. Stare at one long enough and your eyes blur. Find yourself inside one and the walls seem to go up forever. It's like momentum, or gravity, or skating on a lake of ice in the wind. Once you begin, you'll find yourself more likely to continue.

But you don't have to. There is an upward spiral too. Flip a spiral over, and it becomes a mountain. The difference is that you walk on the outside. The difference is that the view from the peak is breathtaking.

You can always turn around and start climbing!

Climbing is more work. It's always easier to walk downhill. You don't even have to walk. Just fall, and gravity does the rest. But trust me, at the bottom what used to feel like freedom, becomes confining when the walls of the spiral start closing in.

What are the first steps in the downward spirals of your life? Are there people that if you hang around them, you will begin your downward trend? Have you just started on that spiral? Turn around and ask yourself what it will take to flip the spiral. You can do it.

Apply this to my head

Where are you on the spiral? (The top, in the middle, at the bottom?)

You can turn around and start climbing. What changes would you need to make to start going in the right direction?

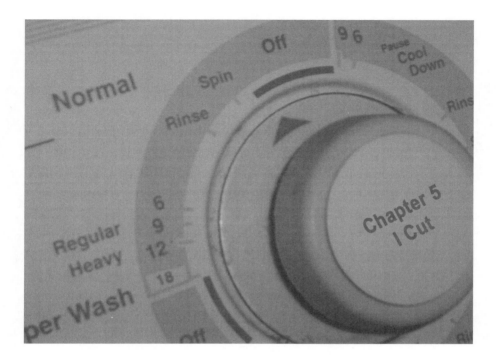

Chapter 5
I Cut

I rented the movie "Walk the Line" the other night. You have to understand that I'm a hard-pounding rock and roll guy down deep, but I found myself getting into that movie. A couple of days later I went out and bought the Best of Johnny Cash C.D. (Don't tell anyone.)

One of the songs that Johnny did in his later years is a remake of the song "Hurt" by Nine Inch Nails. It starts out like this. *"I hurt myself today to see if I still feel. I focused on the pain, the only thing that's real. The needle tears a hole, the old familiar sting. Try to kill it all away, but I remember everything."*

I don't think the song was written about cutting, but it got me thinking about the hundreds of kids I have talked to that cut. They often tell me, when I ask them why they do it, that **it's the only pain that they can control!**

Sarah in Montana told me that she has become so numb to life that she wouldn't know she was alive if she didn't cut. Jeremy in Ohio said that he knows its wrong, but he feels better when he's done.

I have looked in the eyes of so many hurting kids and it breaks my heart whenever I hear stories like that. I'm not going to pretend that I'm some expert on cutting. I'm really not, but I have listened to enough stories to maybe shed a little light on the subject.

I said at the beginning of this book that people will do anything to medicate themselves. I see cutting as another way to self-medicate. I don't understand the relief that comes with cutting your skin, but I know it is a temporary solution.

There's that word again: "temporary."

Cutting eases the emotional pain but doesn't take away the problem.

That's what I'm trying to help you focus on. There are literally hundreds of temporary solutions to problems, but these solutions just make it worse in the end. I see cutting as another temporary solution to a much bigger problem. Just like any other self-medication, you have to cut more to get the same relief as time goes by, which can be so dangerous. Cutting deeper and more often.

Back to Sarah from Montana: She wouldn't know she was alive if she didn't cut. She was that numb. Something deep inside her just shut down. She was not going to let herself feel the emotional pain that was part of her life.

She flipped a switch and went inside herself for protection.

The problem with that is you're still not alone in there. You have your thoughts and the memories that still scream in the silence. For whatever reason, left to our selves, our thoughts can often go "dark" very fast. Some of you know exactly what I'm talking about.

I understand wanting to hide, to protect yourself from being disappointed and hurt again. But I want to help you with a more permanent way to make the pain stop.

In any kind of pain management, you have to find out what triggers it to effectively deal with it.

Jenny from Nebraska told me that whenever she is under stress she feels the need to cut.

Stress can be a trigger. What causes you stress? It might be confrontation with a family member, other people's expectations of you, or poor self-image.

The first step is identifying what triggers your stress. The next step is to find an alternative response to the stress.

It needs to be something you have already thought through ahead of time.

Here are some examples: (Put a check mark by any that might work for you)

___Physical exercise   ___Listening to music
___Painting   ___Journaling
___Taking a walk,   ___Talking to a close friend,
___Shopping,   ___Praying
___Playing an instrument

List some other activities that you could try that might ease the stress in a more constructive way.

We are such creatures of habit that within a few times of doing something different, you can develop a habit of easing stress in a way that doesn't bring harm to you.

For me personally, there are two things that help me. One is praying. I don't pray like I am a monk or something. I talk to God like he is sitting right next to me, sipping on a Coke. It makes me feel better if I can imagine Him as a real friend. I read in the Bible that Jesus is a friend who can be closer to you than your own brother. That sounds good to me.

The other thing I do is talk to a close friend when things get a little tough. I recently went through a hard time with my family. A lot of old feelings and pain resurfaced. I had the greatest talk with my best friend about it. She is my wife. After I was done venting, I felt so much better.

It is very important to have someone like that. Most of you reading this are probably not married, but the point is to have someone you can talk with.

Also, you should never be embarrassed about seeing a counselor or seeking some other kind of professional help. Those people are usually really good at helping people. But like many things, you may have to "shop around" until you find someone you feel you can trust. Find someone you can be yourself with.

I have talked to counselors at key times in my life and it really helped me get over a few hurdles. Sometimes they just help you think of your situation in a different way. We all need that from time to time.

Apply this to my head

Have you ever cut?

If not, do you know someone who does?

Cutting is a form of self-medicating. What are some of the reasons you or someone you know, cut?

There are probably a number of good websites out there on cutting, but there is one in particular that I am impressed with: http://kidshealth.org/teen/your_mind/feeling_sad/cutting.html

I was at a party one night where everyone was drinking. I saw this guy beating up a kid who was definitely smaller than he was. I told the guy to stop; but he didn't, so I grabbed the back of his shirt to pull him off. He got up and punched me in the face.

The next thing I remember is the police pulling me off this kid. Someone told me later that the guy's girlfriend hit me over the head with a beer bottle and I was bleeding. The reason I don't remember any of this is because

I blacked out.

I would get so angry that I wouldn't even know where I was. I really wasn't that angry with the kid I was fighting. I was angry at the world, my dad, my mom, even myself.

Have you ever felt that way, like you were a hundred dollars mad for a fifty-cent problem?

That is the problem with anger. Your anger is not always directed at the people that hurt you. It is usually someone like a family member, girl friend or even your child.

These people have nothing to do with the problem they just suffer from your anger.

For the first half of my life, I wanted to be heard, but the only thing I had to say was how much pain I was in. I was angry, and not just because I felt cheated by life. I was angry because I didn't know what to do about it. I was angry because I didn't have a solution.

Anger is another way that I medicated my pain.

It wasn't so much the angry outbursts that made me feel better, but a constant angry-at-the-world attitude. I hated everything and everyone.

I justified my anger because people usually didn't know how to deal with me, so they played right into it by treating me with disrespect. And the cycle just continued.

It's not too hard to feed anger today. All you have to do is find some people who feel like the world has kicked them in the head, and you draw hatred from each other. There are websites, music, movies and other places that someone can go to feed their anger.

In "White America" by Eminem, he says that he never imagined all these people would feel the same way he does. It doesn't surprise me at all that a lot of young people are angry. **I see it in their eyes.** They have the look of a caged animal.

I recognize it because I used to see it all the time in the mirror. There are thousands of angry kids out there who feel like they have been let down by the very people that should have protected them.

Adding insult to injury, some adults misunderstand and blame teenagers for their anger, assuming they somehow come out of the womb angry.

There are reasons people do what they do.

I am responsible for what I do with that anger, but I am not always responsible for how it got there.

Anger is a fact of life. If you go through this life and never get angry then you probably don't have a pulse. It's just when you allow anger to build and you don't do anything about it that you can have a problem.

The first thing to remember about anger is that it didn't start with anger.

The first emotion you probably felt over an incident was hurt and disappointment. It might have been a long time ago so you probably have to think hard to remember the exact circumstances. For example, I was hurt when my dad left us and then never called.

My hurt turned to anger when my attempts at communicating those feelings were ignored. I felt like people really didn't want to hear what I had to say, that I wasn't important enough. Have you ever felt that way? So I drifted away and got angry, which made people more frustrated with me, which only fed the cycle.

I am considerably less angry than I was when I was young. Rather than addressing the anger, I first dealt with the pain. I went back to the original emotion, which was hurt and disappointment.

I'm not saying you should sit around feeling sorry for yourself. However, I think it is important to let yourself feel the hurt.

I remember someone from my church getting in my face and asking "Why are you so mad? What is driving this anger?" I didn't have an answer. All I could do was cry. I have to tell you, when I let myself feel it and realize that I had a right to be hurt, it was like a huge weight was lifted off.

I think that is the key: Knowing that you have a right to be hurt.

I spend most of my time after assemblies listening to kids tell me all the bad things that have happened to them.

This is about all I say afterwards. "I'm sorry. You are right. You certainly have a right to be hurt. I am so sorry." Sometimes you can literally see the relief in their eyes. Like they knew that they had a right to be angry, but no one ever gave them permission.

I love the movie "Good Will Hunting." I love the part toward the end when Robin William's character tells Matt Damon's character that all the stuff that happened to him was not his fault. When he starts to get it, he breaks down and bawls. Here is this tough kid from South Boston letting himself feel the pain. What an incredible scene. That is when the breakthrough came. When he realized he had a right to be hurt. That it wasn't his fault. I think that is one of the most powerful scenes in any movie I have ever seen.

Sometimes I get frustrated with the fact that our culture says it is not okay for guys to cry or feel pain.

That is simply not true. The strongest guys I know are the ones that have the guts to show emotion. The guys that hold it all in then beat up their girl friend, or wife, or kids behind closed doors are the ones that I think are wimpy. Get some backbone and deal with the pain before it gets that bad.

I'm not going to say that I'm completely anger-free now. I don't think that ever happens, but I can honestly say that whenever I feel myself getting angry, I can usually trace it back to some kind of hurt that I feel and I try to deal with it. We have a chapter on trust and another one on forgiveness coming up. They were real big principles in helping me deal with my anger.

Apply this to my head

What things in your life right now make you angry?

Try and identify the original emotion of hurt, then write it down. It might be more than one event. Write them all down.

Write down in detail how you felt at the time.

Let yourself feel the hurt. Write down how you feel.

Don't be afraid to talk with someone if you need to. Write down a few names of people that you might be able to talk with.

What are some other constructive ways to deal with the anger?

Some hurts are so deep and painful that we need someone, like a counselor to help us deal with them. Also, if you know you are angry but can't pinpoint why, get help! Go to someone you trust who can help you work through it. If, at any time you feel overwhelmed or you are thinking about hurting yourself or others, seek help. No joke. This is serious.

52

Normal

Spin

Off

9 6

Pause
Cool
Down

Rinse

Rins

Chapter 7
I know he
is using me

6
9
12
18

Regular
Heavy

per Wash

Off

"I don't measure up." "I'm not pretty enough, skinny enough." "I'm not good enough". That kind of pain is very real.

Just ask Jenny, the thirteen year-old I met at a function that I was speaking at in Wisconsin. I was speaking that night about significance and where your value comes from. Afterwards, she asked if we could talk. Shortly into the conversation, she started to cry. She said, "Mike this summer I slept with over 14 guys."

I asked her why she had done that and she said, " I just wanted to feel loved, like I was worth something to someone even if it was just for a little while.

Every girl that I have ever met wants to feel like she is worth fighting for.

I don't care how they act on the outside, people will do anything to find that significance and worth. Worth means value. She wants to know that she is valuable to someone.

Our sense of worth and value should first come from our parents. Their unconditional love instills confidence and value. But what happens when love and support is not communicated clearly, or maybe not at all? We go on a search.

If we are not careful, that search can lead us to places that we never thought we would be.

We search for it in other people. We search for it in our jobs, or sports. We search for acceptance. I have had kids tell me that the only reason they had done some pretty stupid stuff was that they did not want to be left out. They wanted people to like them.

A lot of girls look for significance in their outer appearance.

Most girls will tell you they don't like the way they look. Recently, a survey was taken at a national beauty pageant. Ninety percent of the woman polled said that if they could change anything about themselves, they would change their looks. Are you kidding me? They were the most beautiful women in the world and they still didn't like the way they look.

For many women in our society, worth is directly related to their outer appearance.

So as a dad, do I sit my three girls down and see who is prettier and give more attention to her? Of course I don't. Why does our culture seem to do that?

I recently saw a TV program where Tyra Banks wore a fat suit and walked around New York and people ignored her, even when she was asking for assistance. Then she walked around normal and people were practically tripping over themselves to help her.

Unfortunately our society sends a huge message: unless you are good looking, you don't matter as much.

The message is communicated loud and clear that significance comes from the way you look and not from the content of your character.

At a young age girls will start searching for that significance if it is not there at home. It doesn't take long for a girl to figure out that she can instantly medicate the pain of loneliness and low self worth by accepting attention from guys.

My friend Jenny didn't want sex with those guys. She wanted to feel like a princess. She wanted to feel special. Girls figure out at an early age that some guys are willing to make them feel that way as long as there is a payoff off and the pay off is sex in one way or the other.

So what did I tell Jenny? After she told me more about her family life I began to understand why she was looking for love in the wrong places. All the right places were empty wells. Her dad had left years ago and her mom went from boyfriend to boyfriend and some of them had even been sexually inappropriate with Jenny.

I heard once that our self worth is directly related to what the most important person in our world thinks about us, like our parents.

This left Jenny in a bad place. I told her that there are two other important sources of self worth.

I told Jenny that one of the sources for self-worth is herself. I have learned that I have to be my own coach sometimes. I wish people were lining up to tell me how good I am or giving me encouragement on a daily basis. They are not, and I would bet they aren't in your life either.

I wake up everyday and try the best I can. Some days are better than others, but I can look myself in the mirror and know that I am trying. For a guy that grew up without a dad, I'm doing pretty well.

Someone told me once that **right choices bring right feelings.** If you make the right choice, even when you don't feel like it, eventually right feelings will come. Sometimes I hate making the right decision at the time, but I always feel good about myself later.

I started making some good choices, which caused me to feel better about myself, which in turn made me want to make better choices. Most people with low self esteem live in the opposite cycle. They make bad choices, which makes them feel worse about themselves so they make more bad choices. I think you will find that you can reverse the cycle with a few good choices.

I also told Jenny that the most important source of self worth is God. God's love, unlike human love, is unconditional. That means his love doesn't change no matter what. His love can be a huge source of self-esteem. There is a verse in the Bible that says "If God is for us then who can be against us?" If God is for us then it really doesn't matter what other people think.

I have to say that in my life this has been the most important source of worth. As a young kid I realized pretty quickly that I was out of options as well.

I wasn't finding acceptance very easily, I'm not trying to come off preachy here but, I would be lying to you if I didn't tell you that my faith in God and my trust that he really does love me, no matter what I have done, has been an incredible motivator in my life.

My wife wrote a story a couple of years ago for our youth group that illustrates God's love in a way that I can't explain. If the God thing is not where you are at, then substitute the "King" in the story with a future husband or your Dad. If you're a guy reading this story, then maybe you are like me. You aspire to be the kind of dad to your daughters that the king in this story is.

Once upon a time there was a little girl who grew up believing, as most girls do, that she would live "happily ever after". Deep down inside she believed that there was a place where dreams really do come true and that someday

57

all the pieces of her life would fall into place. She wanted to believe that somewhere deep inside her there was a princess, and eventually she would find her kingdom.

Then one day, her fantasy was broken, the castle crumbled, the knight faded away, the dragon won. The little girl knelt at the ruins of her dreams. She knelt there with the heart of a princess, the dignity of royalty and no reality to show for it. Kneeling at the ruins of broken dreams is one of the loneliest places of all. It was in this place that the princess lost sight of her dream completely.

*She lived in this place of darkness for a long time until one day she happened upon her father's house. The place where all dreams are realized. The only place that is completely safe. The princess learned that dreams do come true in this place. She discovers that no matter what has happened in her life, the king still sees her as a princess. Her true identity can only be found in his presence. She doesn't have to be strong...he will fight for her. She doesn't have to be perfect because he never expected that in the first place. She doesn't have to be beautiful for her true beauty is in the strength of her character. She could never be dethroned because there is no one else who can take her place. Her tiara is nothing that she has earned, or even deserves. It belongs to her simply because the king chose to give it to her. Now she must decide whether she will wear it or not. For no matter how tarnished her crown has become, even if it was lost altogether, she has always been and still remains a princess in his eyes. The king, above all others, wishes her story to end...**happily ever after.***

Apply this to my head

On a scale from 1 to 10, how would you rate your self-esteem?

1	5	10
The		Very
Worst		Good

Do you feel pressure to look a certain way?

Right now in your life are you making mostly good, or mostly bad choices?

What good choices do you think you can begin to make?

Chapter 8
Sex isn't
ice cream

I was on a trip to Mexico working in an orphanage. That's when I found it. I was with my friend Jeremy working in a graveyard next to the orphanage when I stumbled across it.

I screamed.

"What is it?" Jeremy asked.

"Dude," I said (we used the word dude a lot back then.) "I found a skeleton."

Apparently, grave robbers had come into the cemetery and looted the corpses. But I wasn't thinking about that. I wasn't really thinking; because I was standing in another country in a graveyard next to an orphanage and a human skull was staring at me.

Skulls freak me out. They're like a book cover with no pages. But they're a weird fascination. I always want to know their story.

We spent the rest of the time while we worked making up stories about John, or Juan depending on the story. He was a cowboy chased down out of Texas into Mexico. He was also a drug runner, a Spanish conquistador, and a guy from Chicago whose parachute didn't work.

But those were the stories we made up. The truth is that once upon a time emotions raced around in that person's head. They loved and lived and did all the things that all of us are doing. They had a story. We don't even know if they were a male or a female. But it doesn't matter; they had a story and if they were to tell it, I bet I know what they would talk about.

And it isn't sex!

Even though you know that's true, it's hard to believe when you're a teenager. If they lived anything close to a normal life, they'd probably talk about what they loved.

Duh, Mike, they would have talked about sex because they probably loved it.

Maybe they did. But imagine it's you. Imagine you're the skull in someone's hand. You lived your life. It's over. Imagine you're telling your story. Are you talking about all the people you slept with? You're not even talking about people you may have been in love with that you had sex with.

You're talking about THE person you loved, THE person you spent your life with. And you might mention sex. It might be a footnote in the story. You might say, and when we made love, I knew that I was safe. I knew they didn't judge me. I knew that there was nothing in the universe I wanted more than to love and be loved.

You would talk about children and family. You'd talk about what you did for a living, the type of person you were and the difference your life made on the earth.

You wouldn't be talking about having sex with someone you dated as a teenager. Even someone you were in love with. Why not? Because it doesn't matter.
You won't put it in your story because it won't have been important to you.

But Mike, it matters to me right now. Isn't that always the dilemma? Have pleasure now or wait and have more pleasure later? And trust me, in the context of a lifelong relationship, sex is so much better that it's almost not the same thing.

I'm not saying that if you have sex as a teenager, your sex life as an adult will be ruined. **But I am saying that choosing to have sex as a teenager can change your life. I am saying that I don't know anyone who regretted waiting until they were adults and thousands who wish they had.**

Sex isn't ice cream! It won't melt if you

don't have it now. It isn't going to go away, and you're not going to miss out. It's been around a long time, and in my opinion I don't think it's going to go away anytime soon.

Reporters and authors always ask themselves this question when they write. Is this crucial to the story? Why introduce something as potentially life altering as sex into your story until it becomes crucial to the story?

I'm not just talking about STDs and pregnancy either. We talked earlier about the power of emotions in our lives and the challenge of handling them properly. Introducing the emotions that come with sex into your life now is simply unnecessary.

Have you already crossed that bridge? You know exactly what I'm talking about then. Remember that it's your story and every story has a script. Whatever direction you've been headed in, it isn't too late to rewrite the script.

I'm not really sure what skulls have to do with sex, except that when it's done right it's more about your mind than your body. It still freaks me out to think that someday someone might hold my skull in his or her hands. I hope the life I lived puts to shame any stories they might conjure up.

Maybe I'll get mine engraved, "Boo", Or across my forehead I'll put "Mike was here."

But I'd rather it said, "He changed his world."

Apply this to my head

What would you want people to say about you as a person after you are gone?

Do you know anyone who regretted having sex as a teenager? Why?

Is having sex crucial right now in your life? Why?

Chapter 9
Country
club skills

On a summer day when I was about thirteen years old, I asked my mom for ten bucks. She started a sermon on the virtues of making my own money and being responsible for my own happiness. Whatever.

I told her that I was too young to have a job, and it was her responsibility to meet my needs. That didn't help. She said that when her brother was thirteen, he would go down to the local country club and caddy for all the golfers; and they would pay well.

That sounded like a good idea; so I called my best friend, and my mom gave us a ride to the country club. I was feeling pretty good about it – until we got there. You have to understand, we looked like "Beavis and Butthead." He was Butthead. Every time we even approached a golfer they stood in front of their clubs in order to protect them from being stolen by us. There was no way anyone was going to let us near their clubs.

I had heard once that you could retrieve golf balls from the ponds on the course and sell them to the golfers for a quarter; so we went down and used sticks to try and get the balls. We had not been there long when, all of a sudden, we heard this guy yelling at us to get out of there.

We went back up to the main part of the country club and noticed that they were setting up tents for a big event. We asked if we could help, and they pretty much sent us the message that they didn't want us there.

I called my mom and told her to come get us, and we walked down to the front gate to wait for her. We noticed that there were a lot of cars coming in for the event. I got an idea. I told my friend, "Let's charge each car fifty cents for parking."

We tried it out on a few cars, and people actually gave us the money! A few people just drove past us, but most of them gave us money; and some people even tipped us!

We collected about twenty-five bucks before we noticed a guy from the country club "hauling the mail" down toward us. Just then my mom came, and we got in the car and drove off. She asked how we did and we said, "Great!"

Have you ever tried to do the right thing, and the wrong thing was easier?

We tried to make money the old fashioned way, but it just didn't work out. It was easier to do something kind of shady and make a few bucks. I think life is a lot like that.

The honest thing is always harder.

A friend of mine blew up his first car. He didn't know you were supposed to check and change the oil. (This is especially important when the car is older than you). What an idiot. Everyone knows that. But how would he know unless he was taught? And who would teach him when his dad decided that his drug habit was more important than his kids?

When I was younger, we often played a joke on girls when a headlight on their car went out. We would tell them to go to the store and buy some "headlight fluid." Obviously there is no such thing as "headlight fluid." Everyone knows that; except for when they don't.

I had a conversation with a friend awhile back. Here's how it went.

Mike, I feel like I'm just taking up space. Like nothing I do matters. It's hard to care about anything when you don't think anything you do really matters.

I reached out and pinched him hard, really hard.

"Owe!" He yelled, pulling away from me. "What was that for?"

I said, "To show you that something still matters to you, even if it's just avoiding pain. Quit making excuses and do something that matters."

That's the problem we all face. When we were three years old we said, "Mommy, watch!" as we spun in a circle or jumped off a chair. We wanted what we were doing to matter. And if we're honest, we haven't really changed that much. We still want what we do to matter to someone.

It is easy to get jealous of someone who is really good at something, like a natural artist or athlete. But I wonder how many basketball players never reach the NBA. I wonder how many great artists never move past the superheroes they drew in middle school.

There is a difference between talent and skill. Talent is something you're born with. Skill is something you have developed. And skill always has a price tag.

Imagine you are a piece of gold. You have value. We can bundle you up, put you in a room and never let anyone look at you again. You have worth; you're still precious; you're gold. But wouldn't you rather be shaped into something both valuable and useful? I'm thinking ROLEX or maybe a wedding ring.

Two-year-old children love it when you watch them accomplish something; even if it is just jumping off a chair or spinning in a circle.

"Daddy, watch!" my children would say. I watched and applauded. I was very impressed with how coordinated they were.

But as they've gotten older, jumping off a chair and spinning in a circle doesn't matter because most people have that skill. (Although, if you can do it when you reach 95, you might get attention with it again!) But this is very different than saying **you** don't matter.

I like the word intrinsic; it means something that is built in. You have intrinsic value; you are precious and always have been. It's in your nature; you were born with it like a talent. You're gold.

What you do with that value is up to you. You might be saying, "What is so special about me? What skills do I have? I'm not very athletic and I don't look like the people on the magazine covers." (By the way, the people on the magazine covers don't look like that either. Photoshop has done wonders for the human body.)

That's what being a teenager is all about. It's when people choose to become a ROLEX or instead, choose to lock their intrinsic value in a vault of regret.

It's not a competition. It's about being a wedding ring. Same gold – and to most people it has the same value – but to a couple of people, their children, and their families, it's even more precious.

Develop the skill of listening and asking questions, and you will never be short of friends. The skill of humor will bring joy to the lives of others. The skill of saving lives will help you have a rewarding life. The skill to fix computers or design buildings will keep you fed.

But developing a skill takes time and patience and hard work. Some people just aren't willing to do it.

I am about to say something that might make you mad. I want you to think about whom you're listening to. I am one of the biggest fans of your generation. I'm one of those adults who truly understands the obstacles you face and your hesitancy to trust that long-term determination really does pay off.

But I have to say that too many of you use that as an excuse not to try. Your fear of failure has kept you from the joy of the game. Some of my best memories in life are times spent developing my skills.

This is going to sound stupid, but failure has become my friend, my teacher. I wish I would have had a dad or an adult mentor to help me develop some skills, but I didn't; so I needed to rely on my mistakes to teach me.

I have fallen on my face so many times it's not funny. I have also done some things in my life that are incredible. Looking back, I can't even believe some of the stuff that I have accomplished. If you told me ten years ago that I would speak to a half million teenagers and be writing a book, I would have laughed at you.

I am so glad that I didn't let failure paralyze me.

I have developed a little slogan I say to myself when I fail at something. **"Quick down quick up."** I might fail, but I don't have to stay down. I get back up, brush myself off and keep trying.

You can't let failure be fatal in your attempt at greatness.

This book is about developing the skill to survive and reinvent your normal. Not only surviving but actually doing something with your life that matters. It's about developing your perspective.

The days of ripping off people at a country club were fun, but they are over. There came a time in my life when I had to grow up and realize that not everyone will be the most talented; but what I do with my skills is what makes me into who I am. I'm not perfect, but I have some skills. How about you?

Apply this to my head

Developing skills requires hard work. Have you developed a habit of taking short cuts?

Everyone wants a life that matters. What are some of the things that are important to you?

What intrinsic value (inside value) do you have?

Have you ever let failure paralyze you? How?

Chapter 10
Who can you trust

Summer was here, and I was very happy to be out of school. I'd just completed third grade, so I thought I was pretty smart. This morning I was really happy, because my dad was coming to get me to take me to work with him. I couldn't wait, so I got up early and waited for him on my front porch.

He was supposed to come at 8:00 a.m. and I was out there by 7:30. He drove a blue and white dump truck that was very loud, so I knew when he was coming. I watched every car come up my hill, hoping each one would be him. By 8:15, I was getting a little impatient but knew he would be there. At 9:00 I was very concerned and started to get worried. My mom kept telling me that he must have forgotten and to just come in. I waited until 10:30 and gave up. He never called to explain why he didn't come.

He just left me sitting there.

It was no secret to people who knew our family that my mom and I had a tough time getting along. We fought about everything. I always felt that she didn't like me very much, and I'm sure she felt like I didn't respect her. But she never left me sitting there.

She stayed in the game.

Some would say that she didn't always play it very well at times, but looking back, I have more respect for her because she didn't bail. I don't know if anyone can play it well in those circumstances. She was raising four kids all by herself.

When it came time to think about forgiving people, it really wasn't that tough with my mom. I understood that her childhood wasn't that great and the principle of "hurt people hurt people" in chapter 12 came into play. But when it came time to forgive my dad, it wasn't easy.

I was taking questions after I spoke at a school last year and a girl asked me, **"How do you trust people after they have betrayed you?"** That is a really good question. How do you keep from getting hard and never trusting anyone again?

Your normal can get real messed up when a family member does something abusive or rejects you.

I have to say that this is not an easy thing to write about. I wish there was some formula to make it all better. To be honest, it is really tough not to want to crawl inside yourself and go into self-protection mode.

As much as we don't like to admit it, we do need people in our lives.

Web Blogs are all the rage. People reveal things in a blog they would never share face-to-face. Entire communities of bloggers have developed. Perusing a blog recently, I read a teenager's much-distressed tirade on the evils of camping.

His rant had nothing to do with mosquitoes, heat, or humidity. It had very little to do with being stuck with his family for a week with no TV to fill the silences. He was distraught because for an entire week, he would be cut off from his blog.

I'll quote:

My stupid parents are making me go camping for a week. If this leads to a capital crime, I'm entirely convinced it will be justified. I can't go a week not knowing what's going on! My parents have no clue how important you all are. You all are my family. They're just my biological life ties. Do they even know I dated Carrie or have any idea what she did to me? I'm going to go insane.

What makes us want to blog? I'm not criticizing it. I think I understand it. There have been many times in my life that I wish I had a blog family to run to. I just wanted to feel heard.

That need we all have to be heard is why we rush right back into relationships that can do more damage. We get kind of healed up a little bit and then trust someone again. Often times we walk right back to someone who hurts us, and sometimes it's even the same person. We then make another vow that we won't trust anyone ever again; until we feel a little better and the pattern continues.

I can't even count the times that my dad promised me or one of my siblings that he was going to come to an event, and he didn't show. I remember one time he finally came to one of my baseball games and afterward made fun of me because I played the position wrong.

Maybe if he was around more often he could have taught me how to play the position. Just a thought. What did I do? I called him again and tried to see him. There were years of that. I would get frustrated and not call for a while; then when I really wanted to see him, I would call him.

Why do we do that?

Our need is stronger than our fear.

Our need to be loved and accepted is stronger than our fear of being hurt. That is why you see patterns like this in people's lives. You would think they would learn and go on, but it's like they can't because we were made to have people in our lives.

Getting back to that girl's question. I told her that I thought the most dangerous word in our world was not hate, but love.

More damage has been done in the name of love than hate.

If you hate me, I will never let you near me. I will put my walls up, and you will never be able to touch me. If you say you love me and I believe you, the walls come down and now you can really hurt me.

No matter how many times you tell yourself that you will never trust anyone again, you will. You might as well face that fact. So what do you do?

You have to balance your need to have people in your life with the need to keep yourself from being hurt.

What has worked for me is not to give my heart to someone easily. Make them earn it. I have to see if someone is trustworthy before I let them have a big piece of my heart. I watch their character. I observe them live their life. I watch how they treat other people.

I will never understand why a girl will give a guy everything he wants sexually before she trusts him.

He may say all the right things, but can she really trust him? When a guy tells me that he wants to prove his love to a girl by having sex with her, I'm like, "Give me a break."

If you want to prove that you love someone, sacrifice for them. Make them the priority. Don't gratify yourself with sex and call that love. Love is tough. Love takes work. It is not an emotion. It is a choice. It means sacrifice for the other person's benefit. Girls, there are a lot of good guys out there who will sacrifice for you and prove they love you. Be patient and don't give up.

One of the guys traveling with me this year is named Jordan. He has been dating a girl for a year now, and they have not kissed yet. I asked him why, and he said, "Mike, every guy in her life, including her father, has said I love you – then took something from her. I want to be the one guy in her life who says I love you and doesn't take a thing."

Girls, that is a guy you can fall in love with.

Guys, that is a guy that you can model after. Jordan is a great athlete and musician, but more than either of those, he is becoming a great man.

I just sat down with my dad a month ago. I talked with him about how I felt about him abandoning us when we were young. I told him that I forgive him, but he is no longer on the pedestal. From this point on, he doesn't get a pass. He has to prove his love like anyone else. He has made a lot of personal changes in his life that are certainly admirable, but the pattern of ignoring his children has remained.

I told him that I know what it means to be a dad now, and it takes work. It's not a title; it is a privilege.

I don't hate my dad. I wouldn't give anyone that much power. I actually really love my dad. I love him enough to tell him the truth. The truth is; if you want me to trust you, then you have to earn it.

Apply this to my head

Do you agree that love can be more dangerous at times than hate?

Have you ever been hurt more than once by the same person?

Why do you think you might let people who hurt you remain in your life?

What are some character qualities in another person that would make them trustworthy?

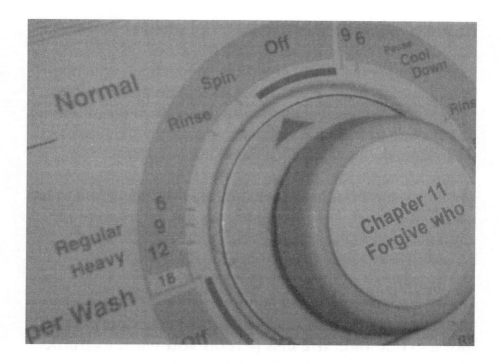

Chapter 11
Forgive who

I was in third grade on my way home from school, and I saw my grandparents' car in the driveway. I started to run home because I was excited. I loved my grandparents. They were always so nice to us. When I got to my yard, I knew something was wrong. My mom was yelling at my grandfather to get in his car and go home. I didn't understand. My grandmother was not there.

The more I looked at my grandfather it became obvious that he was drunk. **What happened next changed my normal when it came to my family!**

I went over to give him a hug and say hello, and he put his hands around my throat and picked me up in the air. My mom was screaming at him and telling him to stop. I couldn't talk because I couldn't breathe.

He was a retired fireman and was very strong. I was seven.

I looked at his face and I could see so much anger in his eyes. I couldn't understand what he was doing. He never even raised his voice at me before. He walked me all the way around to my back yard, carrying me by the throat; then slammed me up against the house.

My mom chased us back there and was yelling at him to let me go. Just when I was about to pass out, he let go of me, and I dropped to the ground. I couldn't cry right away because I was trying to catch my breath.

Have you ever been so mad at someone that even years later, you can't get them off your mind? It's like a cruel joke; the last person you want to think about is them, but it's like they are burned into your brain. I know a way to make that stop.

Forgive them. Wait, don't close the book… keep reading.

Usually the last thing a person wants to do when someone has hurt them is to forgive them. Many people feel that forgiving someone means "letting them off the hook" or saying that what the person did was not a big deal. That is not what forgiveness is.

Forgiveness actually benefits the person who was hurt more than the person who hurt them.

Corrie Ten Boom was a prisoner in a Nazi concentration camp. She suffered terribly at the hands the Nazis. She said,

"Forgiveness is letting a prisoner go free – only to find out the prisoner was you."

In other words, you're the one that suffers the most. Forgiveness goes a long way in helping you to feel better and overcome the hurt and pain in your life. So what is forgiveness?

Forgiveness is taking a hard look at what happened to you. It is not sweeping what happened under a rug or just trying to forget it. It is a painful process but worth it in the end. Forgiveness means pinpointing the original – wrong which is usually not too difficult – but then taking it a step further to really look at what the consequences are in your life.

For example, in the case of my grandfather, after that happened, the consequences were that I didn't trust him anymore; and our relationship was never the same. I felt guilty for him being that mad at me. No one ever talked about it, so I never knew if it was because of something that I did.

To come up with the consequences in your situation, try listing all the ways that the hurtful event has affected you. I cannot stress enough that forgiveness is not just trying to forget the event and pretend it never happened. While you may succeed in doing that for a while, you will still suffer from the consequences.

The only way to deal with pain is to go through it.

Think of it this way… if you had a painful medical condition that could only be healed through surgery, you would experience the pain of surgery in order to be healed from the condition. Forgiveness is like surgery. It is part of the process that brings emotional healing to your life. Hanging onto bitterness usually doesn't cause the person who hurt you any discomfort.

The only person the bitterness hurts is you and the people you influence. Bitterness makes a person miserable.

Forgiveness is choosing to no longer hold the person responsible for the pain you feel in your life. In this way you can move on with your life. It takes a great deal of inner strength.

Mahatma Gandhi once said, "The weak can never forgive. Forgiveness is the attribute of the strong."

This brings us to the next question: How do you forgive?

There is not a simple formula for how to forgive. It is different for everyone. There is also no timetable. Forgiveness takes as long as you need it to. Start by identifying the original hurt and who is responsible. Then list all of the consequences you can think of in your life.

When you feel that you are ready, choose to no longer hold the person responsible for any pain that you experience.

This may mean going to the person who hurt you and honestly sharing your feelings, and telling them you are forgiving them; or it may mean just doing it in your own head and never talking to the person. Some people find it helpful to write a letter to the person who hurt them. This enables the person to get their feelings out, then they choose whether to send it to the person or not.

It's also important to know that the person who hurt you may never take responsibility or acknowledge your pain. It really doesn't matter how they respond. The point is that you have chosen to free yourself from the pain of bitterness by forgiving them.

The important thing is confronting what happened and facing it in your own life.

Remember that some hurts are very damaging; and it may be helpful for you to seek professional help, like a counselor. If you are ever considering hurting yourself or others, please find an adult you can trust – like a school counselor, teacher, pastor, mentor or parent. Find someone to talk to. Do not try to handle it yourself.

I know he was drunk, but I never really trusted my grandfather again after that. I can honestly tell you though: I forgave him for what he did. When my grandfather was lying on his deathbed, I went up to see him. I looked in his eyes and knew that I didn't have any hate in my heart for him. I had forgiven him years before that. I don't know if I could live with myself if he had died, and I had not taken the time to search my heart for forgiveness for him. I hope this helps you.

Apply this to my head

Take a piece of paper and fold it in half. On the left side of this page, write down a list of the things that the person you are trying to forgive did to you. On the right side of the page, write down the consequences of that person's actions toward you.

After you have done that, make a choice of your will to forgive that person for what they did. If you are a person of faith, this is a good time to trust in God to help you forgive them.

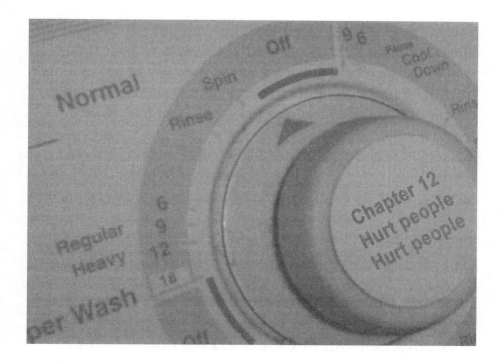

Chapter 12
Hurt people
Hurt people

My mother was not very good at holding her liquor because she rarely drank. Half a glass of beer, and she was toasted. All we had to do was let her sip on a beer, and within an hour she would be heading for bed and out for the night; which worked out great if you didn't want her around. One night, my older sister and brother and I were sitting at the kitchen table, and my mom had, like, three sips of Schlitz Malt Liquor. (Yuck). She was feeling it, so she started talking about her childhood.

What we heard that night changed my normal when it came to dealing with her.

She talked about sexual abuse and abandonment. She talked about what her normal was like when it came to being punished for things. I have to tell you, it was anything but normal.

She talked and talked, and we didn't say a word. I was watching her face and seeing anger and hurt in her eyes as she talked about her father and his abuse and the fact that her mother knew everything but would not intervene.

When she was done she just got up and went to bed. My brother and sister and I just looked at each other. We had no idea. I knew my grandfather drank and got angry once in a while (if you read the last chapter on forgiveness then you know what I'm talking about), but I had no clue that she grew up with so much fear and distrust.

I used to think that my mom hated me. I have come to the conclusion that she doesn't know how to love normally. She didn't hate me. Her normal was messed up when it came to love. She just got really hurt by her parents. This sounds so corny to say, but the old principal that "hurt people hurt people" is true.

There is usually a cycle of pain in families. It gets passed down like an old sweater. Think about your life for a minute. Is there a history of hurt and pain in your family? The cycle doesn't have to continue.

In the case of my mom, it was pretty evident that night when she was talking to us that she still had a lot of pain inside her because of her childhood. She was in her forties at the time, but she was able to describe it as if it had just happened.

I imagine that when my mom and I got into it, and I "pushed her buttons," all the anger and bitterness from her past came out.

It was like her history was talking, not her.

She probably wasn't that angry with me, but when the well got tapped, the anger just flowed. I've certainly seen that in my own life. A small incident can cause a huge water flow of anger to come bursting out.

I'll bet you if you did a little history lesson on the people in your life whom you have been hurt by, you will find a trail of hurt and disappointment in their life.

That doesn't give them an excuse to hurt you, but I think it helps to know where the root of the problem is.

When it came to my mother and I, I carried around all this guilt thinking that I was a bad son; when in reality I was on the wrong end of my mom's hurt. There is no doubt that I was not perfect, but I carried more of the blame than I should have. You probably have as well.

I was determined that when I had kids, they wouldn't have to endure some of the stuff that happened to my mom and I. I didn't want history to repeat itself. The best way for the cycle to stop is to deal with the pain now.

The first step to make the cycle stop was to realize that some of the parenting that I saw on a daily basis was not right. It is important to realize that, because you can't fix what you don't think is broken.

The second step was to actually read some books and talk to people about parenting. I remember when my son was two, he was getting into things, and we had to discipline him. I didn't know what to do; most of the discipline I remember was angry and more like revenge than discipline.

I had been reading some stuff about how to discipline your child so I tried something that I thought might work, which I still do to this day.

Whenever he got in trouble for anything, I would always take time afterward to hold him on my lap and talk with him about what happened. It was cool because no matter how much trouble he got into, I wanted to make sure he knew that I loved him. He's thirteen now, so the lap thing isn't happening; but we still talk all the time.

I'm not perfect by any means, but I have seen that part of the cycle stopped with my kids… It's a pretty cool feeling.

I don't think painful memories ever completely go away, but the sting of those memories will fade with deliberate work and focus on those events that changed your normal. Chapter 11 on forgiveness will help as well.

I want to take an opportunity in this chapter to talk about my family. When you read these stories it might be easy for you to think badly of some of them. I want to assure you that I have the utmost respect for my family.

Talk about reinventing normal: not one of them can realistically tag normal on to their lives, but I have watched over the years my sister Karyn, my brother David and my youngest sister Patricia rise up and do whatever they had to do to make life work for them. I am proud to be a part of this family.

I have to say that now that I am a parent of four children, I have no idea how my mom did it. I hope when you read this stuff that you don't think that I am criticizing her. I have the utmost respect for her. No one is born knowing how to parent. You have to adjust as you go, and I have watched my mom reinvent herself over and over. Thanks, Mom, for putting up with an angry, confused kid. I'm sorry for putting you through all that. And look, I'm writing a book!

Apply this to my head

Write down the names of the people who have hurt you.

Do a brief history lesson on the pain in their lives.
(You might have to ask them about their past)

How does this knowledge change the way you feel about them? (Keep in mind that their personal pain doesn't excuse what they did, but it may open your eyes a little bit.)

Describe the cycle of pain in your family.

What are some ways that you can reverse that cycle?

Chapter 13
My Bad

I was about thirteen years old when some friends and I
decided to take matters into our own hands. Mr. Stanton
was the pedophile in my neighborhood that I talked about
in the second chapter of this book. A few of us had sisters
that this guy messed with, so we decided to make him a
target.

We did everything to this guy. We threw eggs at his house,
called and hung up on him, threw things at him when he
was outside, stole stuff from his yard – anything to make
his life miserable. He was really old; and he had a neighbor
two doors down who would look after him. Mr. Fanning
was about my dad's age. One day I was walking by Mr.
Fanning's house, and he called me over. When I got close
to him, he punched me in the mouth and knocked me to the
ground. He told me to leave the old guy alone.

I tried to explain what he did to my sister, but he wasn't interested. He said, "I don't care what he did; he is an old man, and you need to show some respect." Even though I was pretty mad about being punched in the mouth, he was right. I learned a lesson that day. No matter how victimized I feel, I still have to be accountable for my actions.

I just got off the phone with a friend of mine. She was ranting about her life; how she feels justified to be so cruel to people because she had a bad life.

I told her to grow up!

She said, "What?" I have been her friend for a couple of months now, and she thought she was going to get a sympathetic ear. She went on and on about how everybody in the world has treated her badly. I told her that she was a drama queen, and realistically, there were only a few people that treated her that way. She could avoid them, so she needed to stop whining.

I said, "Stop making your problems everyone's problem."

I think sometimes we feel justified to take shortcuts or treat people like crap because we have had some trouble in our lives. It's a victim mentality that only cripples people in the end. We feel like the world owes us something, and we walk around with a chip on our shoulder. Often times we hurt people that had nothing to do with our pain.

There is something very damaging about being just another spectator and critic in the game of life. This girl that I was talking to is brilliant. She intimidates most people.

She comes off like she knows what she is talking about, because all she does is criticize what everyone else does. She is even right sometimes, which gives her some measure of credibility and most people just back off. I told her she was a wimp. Anyone can be a critic; try playing the game, then you will have my respect.

One of the worst things that I could do for her or anyone else is enable her to be weak by giving her an excuse to sit back and never try. She comes off like she is trying because she is an "expert" on everyone else's life. Not fair.

Moody people bug me. I told this girl that her mood is her master. Whatever mood she is in dominates the situation. If her environment is just right, she is fun to be around. If things are not perfect – let's just say everyone knows.

Anytime anyone calls her on her specific actions, she can give you a long list of reasons why she is the way she is. I wasn't having it. I called her on it because I really do like her. I think she has potential. If she would take responsibility for her own life, her true brilliance would be realized.

That is the key – taking responsibility for your own life. When I try to make it someone else's fault for how I am, I am giving them power that I really don't want to give them. I'm not going to give anyone that much power in my life ever again. I alone am responsible for my life and how it turns out.

That is real power – to honestly say that I can make things better or worse depending on my own actions.

You may be reading this and thinking, what the heck is this guy talking about? Everyday you can wake up and make a choice. No matter what has happened to you, you have the power to make your life better. I could blame my dad, mom, the president, etc… In reality, I am the one who has the choice.

You might be thinking, hey, wait a minute – didn't I just read earlier that I have a right to be hurt? That my pain is valid? It is valid, and you do have a right to be hurt. You also have a responsibility to take that hurt and do something with it. You have a responsibility to yourself and the people around you to not feel sorry for yourself and use that pain as an excuse not to do anything with your life.

The most freeing thing that I have ever done for myself is to recognize and take responsibility for the wrong things that I have done in my life. I have had a history of making excuses for the way I treated people. I remember saying things to my mom that were absolutely hurtful. I can still see the pain on her face after I said those things.

I would try to justify what I said; because after all, she said some pretty mean things herself. The truth is, I could never shake the bad feeling I got when I thought about it.

Freedom came when I took responsibility for what I said and apologized. It really doesn't matter what she did. My words hurt her. That was my responsibility.

I don't have a problem with people who make mistakes. We all make mistakes. We say and do things that hurt others; that is life. The people that bug me are the people who won't own their mistakes. They make cheap excuses and don't realize that by doing so, they are crippling themselves.

Even though I tried really hard not to offend any of my family members with this book; in the first edition, I said some things that offended my mom. At first I got kind of mad, but then I thought about it and realized that she matters to me more than this book.

I went back and reread the parts that were offensive to her, put myself in her shoes, and I got it. I would have been offended as well. I sent her some flowers and rewrote those sections to be more sensitive to her. Mistakes in this life are frequent. People who own their mistakes and make adjustments are rare.

Get in there and play the game. You'll make mistakes. You will disappoint people. You will probably even get hurt. Be one of those rare people in life who doesn't chicken out and just become an expert on everyone else's shortcomings; but take an honest look at your own life. I guarantee if you stop giving yourself excuses and become accountable for your own actions, you will have freedom that most people just dream about.

Apply this to my head

Have you ever thought to yourself that you had a right to treat people bad because your life was hard?

Why do you think being held accountable for your actions, regardless of how you have been treated, ultimately brings freedom?

Are there some things that you have done or said that you have felt bad about, but never really dealt with them?

Write them down and think about some ways you can make it right with the person that you hurt.

Chapter 14
Flip the script

I smoked a lot of pot as a teenager. Mrs. Lawrence called it "marihoochie." I can still hear her voice.

"You're a good boy Michael. Don't you be smoking any of that marihoochie."

She didn't know I smoked pot. She thought I was a good boy. She was wrong on the first part; but right, I think, on the last one.

Mrs. Lawrence was an older lady who lived in my neighborhood. One Wednesday evening as I was sitting in the park across the street from her house, I saw her take the trash out. It took her ten minutes to make the trip from the back door of her house to the curb. She used a walker and was dragging the garbage can.

The next Wednesday I saw her again and tried to help. She told me to get away from her. She was a bit on the cranky and aggressive side. I always liked that. It took me a few Wednesdays, and finally I just took the garbage can out of her hands and carried it to the curb. I could be a little aggressive myself. That's how it started.

Every Wednesday night for three years I went to Mrs. Lawrence's house and took out her trash. At the time, I told myself I was doing a good deed. I'd done enough evil in my life and needed to do some good.

Picture this: a thirteen year-old kid with long hair, wearing a leather jacket, sitting down having a cup of tea with an eighty-year-old lady every Wednesday night. I would stay for over an hour every week.

I washed her rugs for her, did her dishes – even painted her bedroom for her one time. She made me feel trusted. That was one of the best feelings I ever had. I'd have done anything for her just for that reason.

The park across the street from her house was where we all used to party. Mrs. Lawrence would complain about the "punks in the park." She couldn't see much farther than her own hand, so she never knew I was one of them, one of the punks that smoked "marihoochie."

But I was a good kid. She told me I was. She believed I was.

I remember walking home from her house sometimes feeling good about myself, but also feeling like a phony. It was like I was two different people.

The punk in the park felt normal and the kid that helped the old lady felt normal too.

Who was I? It was as if I had two personalities.

Have you ever felt that way? Like you were two people? I know she was half-blind, but why couldn't she see what everyone else saw? They saw the punk in the park. Mrs. Lawrence saw the good kid. But who was I really? I was as confused as anyone.

I like standing in the gym as kids are filing into the assembly programs that we do with R5. They have no clue what is about to happen. They think it is going to be another one of those dumb programs that just bores them to tears and really has no clue about what is going on in their world.

I look at them all dressed up in whatever social costume they are wearing.

You know what I'm talking about...the jocks, goths, preps, emos, etc. Everyone is wearing their identity, or at least what they want us to think.

Have you ever wondered why people are the way they are, though? Like why does someone decide to be Goth, or what makes someone a prep? It is like we get handed this script when we are young. Everyone is required to play their part.

Sometimes it's like you don't even have a choice. If you come from a certain scene then you have to follow that script. If your scene is the trailer park then maybe you don't get that great of a script.

If you are skinny and beautiful, then your script will take you anywhere you want to go. Who writes these scripts? Why do we follow them? Is there any other way of doing it?

I just talked with a kid from Wisconsin today. He said, "I know what you mean about the labels. I've got several of them." My first impression is that he was smart and a little eccentric, and he probably liked heavy metal.

He was tall, dressed in black, and had jet-black hair. I asked him what the labels were that people gave him. He said they call me a Satanist. I said, "Well, are you?" He said, "No, I go to church all the time, and I'm active in my youth group."

He also said that no matter what he tells them they will not believe that he goes to church. Isn't that sad that people had no idea what this kid was about? They looked on the outside at his dark clothes, and handed him his script.

They wouldn't accept anything else.

The sad thing is that sometimes we don't either. It's like we mindlessly take this script and start doing what it says, never thinking that we can be something different; or if we think we can, we don't have the confidence to make it happen. But who was I? Mrs. Lawrence didn't know I had another script. She had the good kid script.

My script was the "Loser." White trash. My dad left; we didn't have a lot of money; our house was run down; our dog was mangy, and our car was always breaking down.

That was the scene, so there had to be a script that went with that. And there was. I felt it.

I was supposed to be the angry kid who gets in trouble all the time, uses drugs and never really amounts to anything. I heard it all the time from everyone. "Michael, you're never going to amount to anything. You're going to be a loser just like your father."

Did they know something I didn't know? How does someone just come out of the womb a loser?

I don't get it. It's like they handed me a script and said, "Here, this is all you get. Look around you; how could you think that you could have anything else? You can't have another script because of your circumstances, okay? Just live with it." The funny thing is I took it. I believed it. For a long time I believed it.

What is your scene? What does it look like? Are you the rich kid who has everything handed to you? You never have to work for anything. Is that your scene? What's the script? The shallow kid who doesn't care about anyone but them self?

Or are you the Christian kid who has parents with a lot of expectations; they hand you a script that looks a lot like a Bible. Do you start writing your own chapters in it that they don't know about? I have a friend of mine whose dad is a "big wig" in a certain denomination, and they think that she is perfect. They handed her the script a long time ago, and she just plays her part. We have the kind of friendship where she can be real with me. I have to tell you, the way she is living now looks nothing like how her script reads.

Maybe your scene is the divorced home. Your script could be angry or sad or depressed. You're the depressed one, and from now on you will always be depressed.

Maybe you don't get good grades so you get the dumbed-down script. "Scripts for Dummies." They tell you that you can't go to college, so you don't even try.

Are you the jock that has achieved success on the court or field? Does your script come with a lot of pressure to always be the best?

Maybe you're the girl who didn't grow up with a dad who made you feel special and worth fighting for. You get your script that comes with a condom and says, "Be the girl that everyone uses because that's where you find love." Whatever the scene is, there is always a set of scripts that go along with it.

Doesn't that kind of make you mad? People are all too willing to just expect you to do what comes along with your scene. Sometimes if you try to write your own script, they don't get it. If you look around and observe life a little bit, you will see that I am right.

People tend to settle right into the expectations that others have for them. I learned that lesson one day in elementary school.

A big chapter in my script was written one day in fourth grade. Up until then I was a D student. I just blew school off. I got in trouble all the time for grades; and even though I didn't show it, I kind of felt bad about it.

I had a great fourth grade teacher. She drew out the best in me. I got good grades for the first time in my life. I remember coming home the last day of school with my report card and some other achievement awards that I had won. I was so excited to show my mom. I was just sure this was going to make her happy.

I got home and showed her. I will never forget her response. She looked at my B's and all that I had accomplished and said, "Well Michael, your sister got A's," and she just handed everything back to me. I couldn't believe it. I was stunned. I felt my heart just sink. I couldn't understand why she wasn't happy about it.

Looking back, I think I know why. My B's were not written in the script. I was supposed to be a loser just like my dad. What was I doing? How dare I go outside the script?

I don't get it, but sometimes it's the people that are close to you who have a hard time with you changing or doing something outside their normal for you.

They can't handle it. It could be because your success is a threat to them, or maybe they have never seen you outside the limitations that they have set. It could be that if you change, then maybe they think they will have to; and they don't want to. For whatever reason, they make it hard for you.

Everybody has a story. Every story has a script. Your parents, your teacher, your best friend – and if you're honest, even you – may already think they know how your story will end. I have spent my life challenging teenagers to rewrite their script, and I don't regret a moment of it.

I have watched too many young people slowly compromise their dreams. As a speaker, I have stood in front of thousands of teenagers and talked about not putting others in a box – not judging people based upon how they look or on one decision they've made. I've cautioned against using labels that forever condemn someone as "a slut, a loser, or a nobody."

Do you know what I've learned, though? Worse than being put in a box by your peers or authorities is when we put ourselves in a box.

Let's try an illustration. Draw a box on the bottom of this page. Imagine it is your heart, the secret place in which only you can know. Write in the box your dream or passion.

Good. Now in the space all around it, write a few words of how key people in your life might describe you that are different from your dream or passion.

Here's a copy of what mine would have looked like in high school as an example.

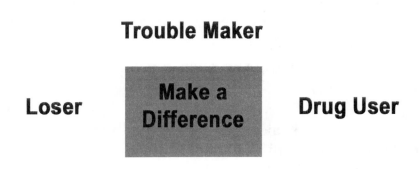

Trouble Maker

Loser   **Make a Difference**   **Drug User**

Disrespects Authority

Buried deep inside me were my dreams, but I allowed the expectations of others and what they believed about me to dictate how I lived my life. Even Mrs. Lawrence's words were drowned out by all the other voices that seemed to be screaming at me.

Every one of us cares about what the people in our lives say and believe about us, and their expectations of us often drive our behaviors. Children who are told they are smart perform better in school. In high school, the overused phrase is peer pressure. But the reality is that the expectations of those around us do act like pressure.

Imagine in the above examples each word or description pushing in toward the center. How can what's really inside get out? Many of us feel trapped by the expectations around us. Our dreams and passions always want to get out, but trapped like this, no wonder so many of them die; and so many of us are skeptics by age 20.

What we need to realize is that the only way to free our dreams is to do something that causes change. Whether it's changing what those around us believe about us or changing the people we surround ourselves with.

But it's easy to talk about change. Actually, rewriting the script is much more difficult and a lot more scary. Many people can't see clearly enough to get the pen to the page, but just admitting your own dreams to yourself is a great place to start; others of you are at the point where you need to take one small step toward your dreams.

Don't underestimate the value of your dreams, and fight "tooth and nail" to keep them alive. When you fight for your dream, the obstacles get smaller and less important.

What do you have to lose besides the labels and limitations that have been crippling you? One small step in the right direction, and you could rewrite the whole thing. You could rewrite your script.

I was about twenty years old when I got a call from one of Mrs. Lawrence's daughters. She wanted me to say hello to her mom who was slipping in and out of coma. The truth was Mrs. Lawrence was close to death, and her daughter wanted to give me a chance to say goodbye.

She got on the phone and asked who I was. I said, "Mike Donahue," and she asked this question; "Did you like me?" It was obvious she didn't remember who I was and that was okay. I got all choked up because I wanted to tell her that she had no idea how much I liked her and how much those Wednesdays meant to me. I didn't know it at the time, but every Wednesday I was able to catch a glimpse of what my script could look like if I had the courage to rewrite it. For one night out of the week I saw myself in a different light.

I hope you can catch a glimpse as well. That's all it takes to get started.

Thank you, Mrs. Lawrence.

Apply this to my head

Have you ever felt like you were two people?

Have you ever felt like you were given a script or a label and you felt pressure to live by it?

Describe your script.

Has anyone close to you had a hard time seeing you outside their "normal"? How does it make you feel?

Make a diagram like I did on page 119. Put your dream in the middle and then write down how other people may see you.

Do you feel the pressure to conform to that? Describe the pressure.

What steps could you take to follow your dream?

Chapter 15
Voices in
my head

Have you ever gone to a big city and seen someone talking to them self? I have. I was in Chicago a couple of years ago, and all of a sudden this guy started yelling at himself really loudly right in front of me. It scared me half to death. I'm not making fun of people with mental disorders; I'm just saying it kind of fascinates me. I think I'm jealous of them in a way. They get to do out loud what I do in my head all the time.

Some people are natural conversationalists. They can talk to anybody. I'm like that. I remember when I was really little my sister took me for a walk, and when we came back I heard her say, "Mom, he stopped and talked to everyone we saw." Some things don't change; I still do that. Others have a hard time until they get to know someone. Below is a letter written by a student when I asked him to write out his dreams.

I don't know what to write. I've been staring at this blank piece of paper for ten minutes. I guess I don't have any dreams. What does that say about me? I must be the guy from the famous cliché, "If you aim at nothing, you'll hit it every time." That sucks. I never wanted to be a cliché. .

All I know is that I want my life to be different than it is now. Sorry, Mike, I don't know what's wrong with me. I couldn't even write this simple letter.

Why was this so difficult for him? I know this guy. He's brilliant. Why would the simple task of writing down the dreams he has for his life be such a challenge?

The answer will surprise you. He needs to work on his conversation skills. It isn't that he doesn't have dreams. It's that he's never talked about them with himself.

What? You want me to talk to myself? What kind of all-knowing guru are you?

I'm not a guru. But I have learned that if we begin to ask ourselves the right questions as teenagers, we save ourselves a lot of pain later. Maybe you're like me – you can talk to anyone except yourself.

Or if you do talk to yourself, maybe you're having the wrong conversations. Maybe you're a bad influence on yourself. Eavesdrop sometime on the conversation. Is your conversation a bitterly sarcastic dialogue about the injustice of the social environment of your school (i.e. are you always ripping on the popular kids)? Or are you your worst critic? Is your conversation a one-sided review of all your shortcomings?

As I travel this country speaking to students, my job isn't to give them some eye-opening piece of information they didn't already know. It's to get them to listen to what's already in them. In fact, I spend most of my time helping them unlock the doors and tear down the walls of their hearts. Because the answer was always right there. Many times it's getting them to take an honest look at the lies they tell themselves. Do you know how many young people blame themselves for their parent's divorce?

Is a 10-year-old really responsible for their parent's divorce? Do they really have that much power? Of course not!

Think about your life for a minute. How many lies have you bought into that swim around your head on a daily basis? Lies about your weight, your looks, your personality etc. Are you really the ugliest girl in the world? Are all the problems in your family really your fault?

Psychologists say that we talk to ourselves at a rate of 1,100 words per minute. A natural conversation with someone is about 300 words per minute. In fact, it is quite realistic that while a conversation is going on with someone else, we are talking to ourselves at the same time. At 1,100 words per minute a lot of negative stuff can get in there, and we don't even know it.

It is very important that we filter what is being said to ourselves. As a parent, I am very careful about what is being spoken to my children. We are constantly filtering what they hear because they are so impressionable. I don't want them to be damaged by something someone – a teacher, a pastor, even some of their friends – says to them.

We have to be just as diligent at filtering our own thoughts. I want you to try a little test. For the next couple of days keep a notebook close to you and write down random thoughts that come into your head that are negative about yourself. Write it down as much as you think it. Then take the list; and on the left side of the paper, rewrite the thought. On the right side of the paper, filter that thought with reality.

For example, mine would look something like this: on the left side would be born to fail; on the right, I would look at that and honestly say that no one is born a failure. I can change my circumstances by my own choices.

To do this, sometimes I have to take myself out of the equation. I have to pretend that I am looking at someone else's list. I can be a lot more objective if it's not mine. In other words, the logic and truth that we would use to help someone else is what we need to use for ourselves.

Problems arise when the lie gets proven, so when presented with the truth, we think that the lie is the truth and the truth is the lie. One of my lies, like I said, was that I was just born a loser, so I should not even try because I will just fail. The lie was reinforced when I would fail at stuff. I had a long history of quitting and failing at things. The lie was pretty deep. One of my mentors Jeanne Mayo, who was a youth leader in our church, saw this and would put me in situations that I couldn't fail. She set it up so I would win. Eventually I got the confidence I needed to stop quitting and go after my dream.

Those lies were replaced with the truth that winning and losing is a choice. I learned that I like winning.

I have done this in other people's lives as well. A couple of years ago, we had this girl on our team who was convinced that she had nothing good to say that would help anyone. That lie was started by her father who degraded her constantly. She would say, "I will go to the assemblies and set up and stuff, but don't make me talk up front or with girls afterward." I would ask why, and she would say that she had nothing good to say.

What do you think I did? I put her up front as much as could. I made sure that no one else was able to talk to certain girls, so she would have to. She was amazing. I watched those lies crumble at the weight of her incredible wisdom and compassion. Even she couldn't deny it; and she has now chosen a career in helping other people sort out the lies in their heads. Isn't that ironic?

The real truth is in you. It has been there the whole time. There is a quote that goes something like this: *What you dwell on, you eventually will become.* I'm choosing to dwell on the positive stuff. I invite you to do the same.

Apply this to my head

Try doing what I said on page 128. Take a note - book with you and write down any random negative thoughts that come to your mind about you. Write them down as much as you think them.

Take the list and rewrite the thoughts on the left side of the paper. Examine each thought one by one.

Take the time to really think about each thought. Is it really true? Is it partially true? Which means it is partially not true.

On the right side of the paper, write down the truth about that thought. Try to be as objective as possible. Try and put someone else in the scenario.

After you have shed some truth on those lies, stop yourself every time you start to think about that situation and tell yourself the truth. It works, I promise. The truth is very powerful!

I have to admit that one of my favorite things to do in life was to antagonize my next-door neighbor, Harold. We would get behind his garage and throw rocks at him while he was bent over working in his garden. Or we would sneak up behind him and scare him half to death.

One night my sister and I called him in the middle of the night and breathed heavily into the phone. I think we scared him, because after about the tenth call he put his light on in his room.

Let's just say I was not one of his favorite people. Imagine that. One day my friend Wayne Clayton and I were harassing him when, all of a sudden, he came booking out of his garage with a pitchfork. We had never seen him this mad. I took off into my yard as fast as I could and turned around to see Harold hurl that pitchfork at Wayne like he was throwing a javelin in the Olympics. That thing just missed Wayne by about six inches. I knew we had crossed a line, but that was kind of scary. He could have killed him!

Wayne disappeared into his house. I sat on my front steps letting things calm down a bit. All of a sudden, Wayne's dad came storming out of the house toward Harold's garage. Uh-oh, a showdown! An eighty-five-year-old man against an irate forty something dad. Just the thing I needed to spice up my Saturday afternoon!

Wayne's dad grabbed the pitchfork out of the yard and walked into Harold's garage. We followed hesitantly behind him. Wayne's dad asked Harold if he threw this pitchfork at his son. Harold said, "You bet your a__ I did." Wayne's dad said, "I don't care what these boys did; you have no right to try and kill them. What's wrong with you, you crazy old geezer?" He called Harold an old geezer! This was turning into a great day.

Harold starting yelling and cussing at Mr. Clayton, so he did something that I didn't expect. He slapped Harold's glasses off his head. I couldn't believe it. A good stiff wind would blow Harold over, so I was really surprised that Mr. Clayton did that. As we were all walking away, I heard Wayne's dad say something to Wayne that I will never forget.

"We are Claytons. You don't have to put up with that."

I remember that day like it just happened. It left an imprint on my brain. Not because Wayne's dad almost took Harold out, although that was pretty intense. It was what he said to Wayne. "We are Claytons. We don't have to put up with that."

At that moment I was so jealous. I wanted to be a Clayton. Rather I would have liked it if my dad had said, "We are Donahues. We don't have to put up with that.

My whole life I have felt like I have been on a search to be a Clayton, and to belong to something that I could take pride in being a part of. I have done so many things that I am not proud of, all in the name of trying to belong to something or someone that will make the pain of loneliness go away.

Maybe that's you. You're trying to belong to something. You want to be a part of something that is bigger than you, something that can provide safety and comfort when you need it. Being forty-something myself now, I have learned a few things about loneliness.

I am as lonely as I want to be.

Have you ever heard the phrase "To have a friend, you need to be one?" That is a good principle. Basically, if you give that kind of love and friendship to people it comes back to you. I can sit around and feel sorry for myself that my dad was not there, or I can do something positive in someone else's life because I know what it feels like to not belong.

One of the greatest mentors in my life was a guy named Rick Lorimer. Rick was a real friend because not only was he there in some of the tough moments, but he was also willing to tell me the truth even if he thought it might hurt our friendship.

I'll never forget when he looked me in the eye and said that I felt sorry for myself too much, and that it was keeping me back from my potential. I was kind of mad because he was right. Then he said something that again was one of those things that will stick with me for the rest of my life.

He said, "Mike, you have a choice. You, no doubt, have had a pretty tough life. So you can do one of two things.

You can feel sorry for yourself and quit, or you can <u>give your pain purpose.</u>

Feeling sorry for yourself won't bring your dad back. You can't change your past but you can give it purpose by being there for other people who might feel the way you did when you were growing up."

The more I thought about it, the more it made sense. Then I started to put it into practice, and it changed my life.

One day I got a call from a very upset mother of a kid with whom I had been working with. She was screaming into the phone that her son was bleeding and asked if I could come over. Needless to say I hit the door and headed to his house. When I got there, Jason had a bandage wrapped around his wrist. He had gotten really mad and smashed his fist through a window.

As I drove him to the emergency room we talked. After they stitched him up we talked some more. I could tell I was getting through to him. I was saying some of the things I would have wanted to hear back when I was a teenager. On my way home from dropping him off I had this sense of accomplishment. I dug down deep from my own experience and helped this kid. I'm not saying I'm the next Mother Teresa, but it felt good to see hope in a young man's eyes.

Maybe you can do that too. You can take what happened and turn it into a positive. Maybe you can find a way to share your story so it will help people. You could volunteer as mentor for a younger kid. You could visit an elderly person in a nursing home. There are so many things that you can do to get your mind off your pain and reach out and help others.

When I was twenty years old, I was invited to a youth group right out side of the base that I was stationed at. I have to admit the only reason I went was the girl that invited me was drop-dead gorgeous. If she invited me to hell that night, I probably would have gone with her. I had never seen anything like what I saw. There were over three hundred teenagers and young adults there to worship God. My experience with church prior to this was limited to an occasional Christmas and Easter appearance, so this was quite a bit different.

I went to the group for about six months then lost interest. I went back to medicating pain with alcohol and whatever.

One night when I was in a bar with the girl whom I had been seeing, her ex-boyfriend came in the bar, and they left together. I was pretty upset. It was a Wednesday night, so I drove down to that youth group. I wanted to talk with someone; but I was pretty drunk, so they just escorted me to the door. The guy that walked me to the door was six foot, six inches so I went quietly.

The next day the guy called me and asked me to go to lunch with him. I thought that was pretty cool. He didn't have to do that. I ended up getting involved with that youth group. I interned as a youth minister there and eventually took over the group that I went to drunk. That's pretty cool too. In those years those people became my family. Not everyone that goes to church is like these people.

I was incredibly fortunate that I ran into Christians that were actually like Jesus.

I finally belonged to something that was bigger than myself. I felt acceptance and love like I never had. That church became very important to me. I met my wife and was married there. Two of my children were dedicated there. I met three of my best friends whom I still talk to regularly at that church as well.

I also have grown in a faith that compels me to use my gifts and abilities to reach out to people who are going through similar experiences that I have had. That is why we started R5.

I lost touch with the girl that originally invited me to that group, but if I could talk to her I would say thank you for introducing me to a path that has brought so much normal back into my life. I'm not discounting anybody else's experience with faith. I respect everyone's path. I'm just grateful that I found mine.

My eleven year-old son was in the principal's office the other day for getting into a fight. I had told him that if this one kid kept picking on him, then he needed to take care of business. He tried to get out of the situation, but it became necessary for him to get a little physical. When I came into the room, he was being lectured by the principal, and he was crying. The other kid had an ice pack on his face, and I have to admit I was kind of proud of my son. Keegan thought he was in big trouble with me, that's why he was crying.

We were walking out to my car because he was suspended and he just looked down on the ground. I asked him this question. I said, "Who are you with right now?"
He said, "You." I said, "Who am I?"
He replied, "You're my dad."
"That's right, who else am I?"
He was getting it. He said, "You're my friend."
Smiling, I said, "Right again."

Then I added, "With that in mind you have to remember… We are Donahues. You don't have to put with that."

"There is nothing you can do that is going to make me stop loving you, ever. Do you understand that?"
He nodded, and we went and got a Coke and laughed together as I told him the story about Harold and his pitchfork.

Apply this to my head

Have you ever been jealous of someone else's family? Why?

Do you agree with the statement "in order to have a friend you must be someone's friend"?

Has self-pity kept you from reaching out and making a difference in someone else's life? How?

Write down some ways you can give your pain purpose.

Chapter 17
I hate Christians

She sat across the room from me and had this blank stare on her face. We were getting ready for another year of doing R5 assemblies in public schools. Our team of about fifteen people was sitting in a meeting, as we do at that time each year.

We talk about the coming year and our vision to help students around the nation. Brook, one of our most talented team members, looked like she was bored. I was getting a little irritated. We needed her, and we needed her heart in this meeting.

Every year at the end of the meeting, I look each team member in the eyes and ask them what areas in their life they need support; what they think they will struggle with the most this year. Our goal is for every member of our team to grow in the same ways we challenge students around the nation.

It's a special time for our team because we get close to each other when we share our personal stories. In many of our school programs we say that everyone has a story, and every story is important. We wouldn't be real if we didn't practice what we preach with each other.

When I ask this question, some of them say they are their own worst enemy because of the dumb choices they make. Others talk about the past and ask the team to help them stay away from drugs and alcohol. Some ask for help making better relationship choices.

This is one of the best times of the year for me because we really get close with one another. It's even better at the end of the year when you see them make progress in the areas in which they wanted to grow.

I got in front of Brook, looked her in the eyes and asked, "What are you struggling with and how can we help you?"

She put her head down for what seemed like an eternity. She wouldn't look up at me. I kept waiting and rewording the question so it would be easier for her to answer. I looked down at the floor and saw tears dripping from her face.

I felt bad, but I knew I had to get her to say it. We can't, as a team, have her back if we don't know what we are fighting. She finally looked up at me and said,

"I hate Christians!"

I have to tell you; I wasn't prepared for that. When I tried to get her to explain what she meant, she kept saying it over and over. "I hate Christians. I hate Christians."

You could see by the pain on her face that there was a lot more to it than she was willing to talk about in that meeting. In the following year, piece-by-piece, I came to learn how this young, talented girl became so bitter toward a group of people.

I share this story with permission.

When Brook was fifteen years old, she was your typical teenager. She was on the tennis team; she took ten years of piano lessons; she had, what appeared to be, good friends; and she went to church every Sunday morning and Wednesday night.

Like a lot of people, her parents were having problems getting along. She confided in a youth worker who was eleven years older than she. The man, who was training to be a youth pastor in a major denomination, manipulated her into having sexual encounters with him.

Prior to this point Brook had never even kissed a guy. She said they didn't go all the way because he was afraid that she would get pregnant. He would often play worship music in the room when they were together; convincing her that God wanted this, and that he was really in love with her.

Is it any wonder her feelings about people of faith were distorted?

When others started getting suspicious, the youth leader backed away from Brook. When some of the officials from the church were asked questions, the focus went on Brook. They blamed her for causing problems.

Here was their chance to bring justice and truth to a very painful situation. Instead, to avoid embarrassment, they began to leave her out of things. When it came time to play in the band or sing a solo, they didn't call. They sent her a clear message: **you are not wanted here.**

With things going from bad to worse at home, there was nowhere to go. Betrayed by the youth leader and her church, she started using drugs and hanging out with some pretty shady people. When I met her she was two years into a drug and alcohol addiction. She was self-medicating.

I didn't write this chapter to invoke feelings one way or the other toward Christianity or any particular faith. So much of our perspective, and rightly so, comes from our belief system. I couldn't write a book about reinventing normal and leave faith on the sideline.

Sometimes pain and difficult circumstances fog our vision. The faith that was so clear to us can become clouded. The belief system that once gave us strength may now bring more questions than answers.

I happen to be a Christian, which made it a little awkward when Brook said she hated me.

But I know how she feels. There are people of faith that do honorable things, and their lives are a walking testimony of their faith. And there are some who give their faith a bad name. Guys like Brook's youth leader, who used her faith and his position to manipulate her.

Unfortunately, people like this often get the attention of the press. Look at the Muslim faith, which is filled with kind and caring people who would never kill or use terrorism as a weapon. Most Christians I know don't hate homosexuals, but it is always those ignorant people holding signs in protest that get on the news.

Brook once told me the worst day of her life was when she went with her church for college days to the Bible College that her former youth leader was now attending. He completely ignored her. All the love and loyalty he promised was out the window when he wasn't able to be physical with her. She said that she sat in the back of the van and cried the whole nine-hour trip home.

No wonder faith got a little blurry for Brook. She had only been fifteen. He was in his mid-twenties. Fifteen isn't that far from twelve, when she still played with dolls and had crushes on the "Backstreet Boys."

Of course her normal changed when it came to God. Where was the justice? If the guy were at fault, why didn't God nail him? If he were such a loving God, why would he let

147

her get used by someone in the church? Those are tough questions and ones that don't always get answered right away.

Brook moved into our house shortly after that meeting and became good friends with my wife, Andrea. After many nights of talking and crying with Andrea and me, she began to rebuild what had been damaged.

The feeling that God had abandoned her was very real, but not true. The hardest thing for her to realize was that just because some people of faith aren't always true, that didn't mean that God wasn't. She had to get to the point where she could separate people of faith from the God of her Christian faith.

If you're reading this and your faith has been damaged, don't give up hope. Your vision might be blurred, and questions might flood your heart; but you will come out on the other side.

Last spring, I cried as I watched Brook, a beautiful young bride, walk down the aisle of a church to be married to one of the greatest men of integrity that I personally know. I can't tell you how much joy was in my heart. When she stepped up and took his hand it was like everything became crystal clear. This is real faith. Hate can become love, and wounds can really heal.

The youth leader who went to Bible College isn't doing church work today. Brook is now a full-time youth minister. Oh, and she doesn't hate me anymore either.

Apply this to my head

How has your interaction with people of faith changed the way you look at God? (This can be positive as well.)

Are you able to separate the actions of people of faith from your perception of God?

Someone told me once that the most important thing about you is what you think about God. Take some time and write down how you feel about the whole God thing. You might be surprised how much you really think about it.

150

Chapter 18
Chasing Harold

I laughed a lot as a kid.

You might be surprised to hear that because of all the sad stories I've told. However, I do remember laughing a lot. Stupid things made me laugh.

One time we were driving down the street in my mom's sixty-five Ford Fairlane Five Hundred. (Sounds like a hot car but it wasn't.) All four of us kids were sitting in the back seat. We did not have our seat belts on. I don't think the thing had seat belts. If it did they were stuffed so far down in the seat that they were never coming out!

I wish we were able to find the seat belts because this car had developed a "special feature." **The doors would open up when we went around a corner or went over a bump. I'm not kidding!**

We would hold on to each other for dear life when she hit the corner. My mom would yell out "Hold on!" and we would just grab on to each other. The door would open, and when it was safe one of us would reach out and shut the door.

One of my sister's friends actually fell out one day on the way to take her home! We forgot to tell her about the doors. I bet she wished she would have walked.

My mom got rid of that car shortly after it developed that special feature.

The funniest and oddest things came from old man Harold. He was always doing the craziest stuff. When I was really little he locked me in a room with a live lobster. I just remember him laughing his head off and me screaming mine off.

He had a bull whip in his garage that he would take out when we got near his property. We used to get right up on the line so he would crack that thing at us. He never hit us, but he came really close. (He would "do time" for doing that today.)

One day Harold took my baseball because it went into his yard. He said we couldn't have it back; and I didn't have another ball, so something had to be done. I went into his garage and took some tools. He called the police, and when they came I explained the situation. What happened next was unbelievable.

The police officer made us exchange the ball and the tools at the same time. I felt like I was in kindergarten, except there was an eighty-year-old man staring at me instead of another kid.

Then there was the time that Harold chased us. He was sitting in his back room watching the Boston Bruins play hockey on television. He had these huge windows in that room. My friends and I sneaked into his yard and pounded on the windows. He jumped up ten feet in the air – scared half to death, I'm sure.

The chase was on.

Of course we had to wait ten minutes for Harold to get his hat, boots, coat, and flash light. As soon as he came out the door, though, we took off as fast as we could.

Harold was just walking, so we were well up ahead of him. We decided to cut through some yards and backtrack. We walked up behind him and asked what he was doing. He said he was chasing some kids because they were little terrorists.

We told him that we would help him and started walking with him. We spotted my little brother and his friends. Being neighborly, we chased them down and dragged them back to Harold. You can imagine the shocked look on their faces when Harold lectured them and took down their phone numbers on a pad of paper he had brought with him. He thanked us and gave us a couple of bucks for ice cream for helping him. He actually muttered out something like there should be more kids like us.

Those were some of the best times I ever had. There was just something about that old guy. He had spunk. He was our enemy growing up, but deep down I admired him.

His eyes never died.

You know what I'm talking about. When people have given up and taken the path of least resistance, their eyes die. Harold was alive every day, and getting the most out of life. I'm sure his normal changed a lot throughout the years, especially being a war veteran.

In a strange way it seems like my whole life I've been chasing Harold. I want to live like that. I want every day to be an adventure. I don't want to rot away in a nursing home, wishing I had taken more risks when I was younger; only to die in my sleep one night with a bunch of regrets as my legacy.

I want to be able to look back and know that I didn't take the path of least resistance. I didn't give myself an excuse not to live, love and be loved. I want to look around my room in that nursing home at all the pictures on the wall full of laughter and friendship and devotion. They won't be stained with regret and missed opportunities.

Too many people let life happen to them. They become victims of their circumstances. They justify squandering their lives because their circumstances were tragic.

I can match stories with just about anyone, but I won't do that. I won't give myself an excuse to quit living and just exist.

Meet me tomorrow, in ten years, or when I'm ninety. Look me in the eyes. I dare you! They won't be dead. I will reinvent my normal as many times as it takes. I'm never going to give up getting the most I can out of this life that God has given me.

How about you? Are you ready to keep fighting? I hope so!

If you read this book, I would like to know what you thought. Go to:
Myspace.com/reinventmynormal

or email us at:
Reinventmynormal@aol.com